a walk with St. Francis

18 Days of Readings & Reflection

From the Feast of the Stigmata
to the Feast of St. Francis

Cricket Aull, OFS

Tau Publishing

A Walk with St. Francis
18 Days of Readings and Reflection
From the Feast of the Stigmata to The Feast of St. Francis
Cricket Aull, OFS

Copyright © 2013, Cricket Aull, OFS, All rights reserved

Cover image: Sr. Linda Campbell, OSB
Cover and book design: Tau Publishing Design Department

Scriptures are taken from *The New American Bible* St. Joseph Edition

All Quotes and stories from and about St. Francis were taken from:
St. Francis of Assisi, Writings and Early Biographies, English Omnibus of the Sources for the Life of St. Francis. Trans. Raphael Brown. ed. Marion A. Habig. Chicago, Illinois: Franciscan Herald Press. 1983.

No part of this book may be reproduced, stored in a retrieval system or transmitted in any form or by any means — electronic, mechanical, photocopying, recording, or otherwise — without written permission of the publisher.

For information regarding permission, write to:
Tau Publishing, LLC
Attention: Permissions Department
4806 South 40th Street
Phoenix, AZ 85040

ISBN 978-1-61956-139-7

First Edition July 2013
10 9 8 7 6 5 4 3 2 1

Published and printed in the United States of America by Tau Publishing, LLC, an imprint of Vesuvius Press Incorporated.

♻ Text printed on 30% post-consumer waste recycled paper.

For additional inspirational books visit us at
TauPublishing.com

Preface		i
A Walk with St. Francis - **An Introduction**		vii
Day 1	The Stigmata of St. Francis	1
For Our Love of God		
Day 2	Seeking Solitude	9
Day 3	The Beauty of God	11
Day 4	The Worth of Divine Love	13
Day 5	Faithful Service	15
For Love of Poverty		
Day 6	Clearing Away Obstacles	19
Day 7	Poverty's Surrender	21
Day 8	The Riches of Poverty	23
Day 9	A Humble Dwelling for God	25
For Love of the Cross		
Day 10	Sharing the Needs of Others	29
Day 11	Bearing Sister Suffering	31
Day 12	Practicing Perfect Joy	33
Day 13	Directing Our Efforts to God	35
For Imitation of Christ		
Day 14	Growing in Virtue	41
Day 15	Purity and Spiritual Joy	43
Day 16	Intimacy with Christ	45
Day 17	Living Our Blessing	47
Day 18	The Feast of St. Francis	51

Preface

On September 17, 2012, the day Franciscans celebrate the Stigmata of Our Holy Father Francis, I was inspired with the idea to write *A Walk with St. Francis* - readings and reflections for prayer, beginning with St. Francis receiving the stigmata until his feast day on October 4th. I immediately liked this thought, and even remember thinking, "This is such a good idea, why hasn't it been done before?" Then I proceeded to look for particular readings about St. Francis to which I could add reflections and prayers. Much to my surprise, as I attempted to do this, I could not get even one day ahead in ideas or writing. Each morning prayer time revealed its own reading and reflection for the day, I could not get 'ahead of myself' even when I tried. So, the pages you read here were simply a part of my own 'Walk' between September 17 and October 4th. Of course, this book can be read at any time of the year. My prayer is that you are blessed and inspired, as I certainly was in writing it.

Please do not run
through this book.
It is a walk. Take your time with the stories, with the
reflections, and the prayers. Take time with the words
you are reading, and let yourself stop to ponder what is
being said for you to hear. Just as Francis would want us
to receive the
many and good
riches God has
for us in holy
poverty, please
take your time,
so as not to
miss the many
riches of this
walk, and may
God grant you
PEACE.

A Walk with St. Francis
An Introduction

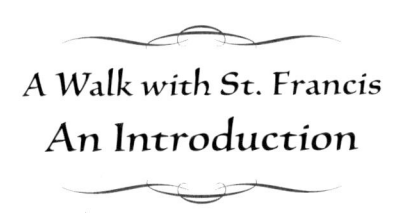

Readings and Reflections to prayerfully use from the Feast of the Stigmata to Francis' Feast Day (or any other days).

Anyone who embraces the call to the Secular Franciscan Order, or, Ordo Franciscanus Saecularis, (OFS), comes to understand that they are choosing to live the gospel life knowing that the lives of St. Francis and St. Clare have set for us an example that will continuously inspire, teach, and encourage us along the way.

It was explained to me once that every founder of an Order was given particular charisms to live the gospel life; and every follower of that founder lives 'under the umbrella,' so to speak, of those same charisms. So we, as Franciscans, are given a call to live the gospel in the footsteps of St. Francis; and with that call from God comes the very graces and gifts we need in order to do this. Every grace we need, for every need we have, is available to us so that we can embrace the charisms that allowed Francis to live this way of life.

It is true that there will be differences in our personal experiences, in the circumstances, relationships, trials and achievements of everyday life, but at the heart of our call to live this holy way will be our own personal imitation of Christ. Let us look to St. Francis, then, whose "true love of Christ" allowed him to be transformed into Christ's image. And let us pray on this journey that we will embrace with deeper gratitude, love, and fervor, what God is doing in our own lives to transform us into the Son's image.

Each day's reading and reflection provides a small step in following St. Francis. As you read these stories about his life there may be specific lines or phrases that touch your heart. I encourage you to let the Holy Spirit speak and highlight and reveal what is meant especially for you. Consider what thoughts and images from Francis' life might become your own prayer for the day. Let us learn from St. Francis and be inspired by his holy example, and

>Let all be done to the glory of God.

Day 1
The Stigmata of St. Francis

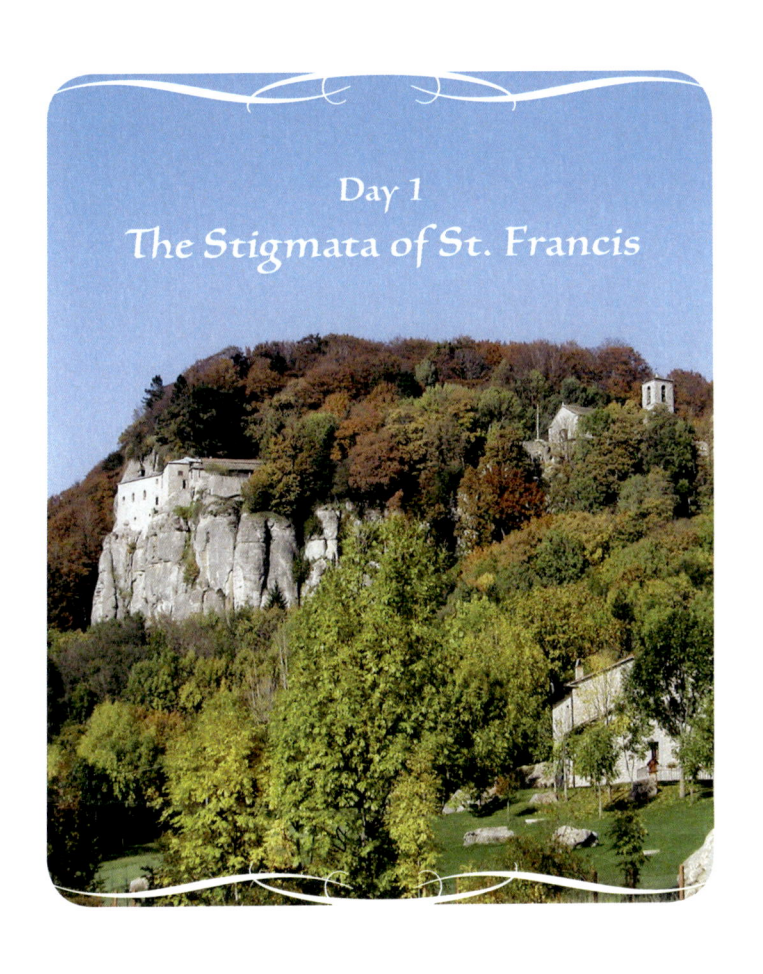

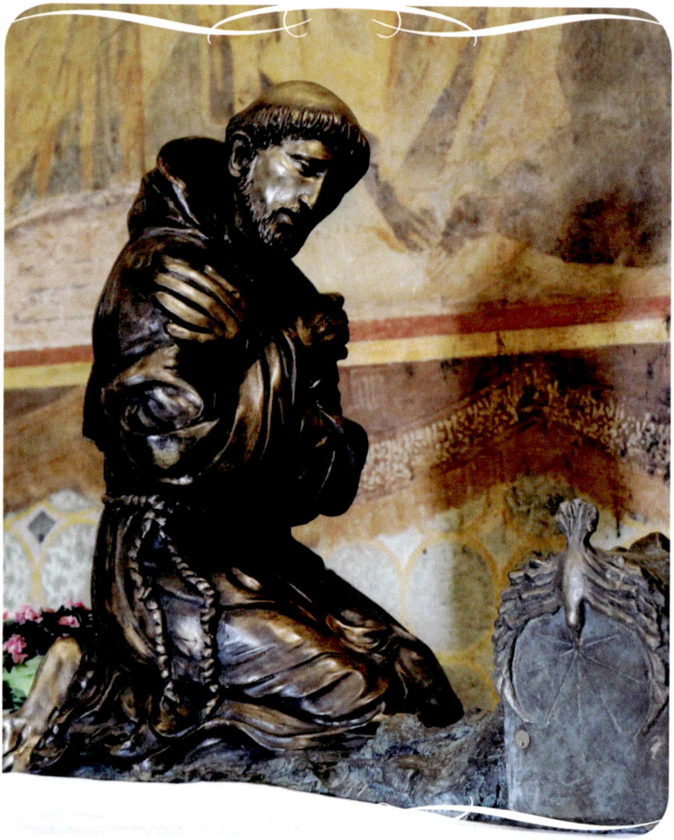

Day 1: The Stigmata of St. Francis

From St. Bonaventure we read:

The fervor of his seraphic longing raised Francis up to God and, in an ecstasy of compassion, made him like Christ who allowed himself to be crucified in the excess of his love. Then one morning about the feast of the Exaltation of the Holy Cross, while he was praying on the mountainside, Francis saw a Seraph with six fiery wings coming down from the highest point in the heavens. The vision descended swiftly and came to rest in the air near him. Then he saw the image of a Man crucified in the midst of the wings, with his hands and feet stretched out and nailed to a cross. Two of the wings were raised above his head and two were stretched out in flight, while the remaining two shielded his body. Francis was dumbfounded at the sight and his heart was flooded with a mixture of joy and sorrow. He was overjoyed at the way Christ regarded him so graciously under the appearance of a Seraph, but the fact that he was nailed to a cross pierced his soul with a sword of compassionate sorrow.

He was lost in wonder at the sight of this mysterious vision; he knew that the agony of Christ's passion was not in keeping with the state of a seraphic spirit which is immortal. Eventually he realized by divine inspiration that God had shown him this vision in his providence, in order to let him see that, as Christ's lover, he would resemble Christ crucified perfectly not by physical martyrdom, but by the fervor of his spirit. As the vision disappeared, it left his heart ablaze with eagerness and impressed upon his body a miraculous likeness. There and then the marks of nails began to appear in his hands and feet, just as he had seen them in his vision of the Man nailed to the Cross. His hands and feet appeared pierced through the center with nails, the heads of which were in the palms of his hands and on the instep of each foot, while the points stuck out on the opposite side. The heads were black and round, but the points were long and bent back, as if they had been struck with a hammer; they rose above the surrounding flesh and stood out from it. His right side seemed as if it had been pierced with a lance and was marked with a livid scar which often bled, so that his habit and trousers were stained.

    St. Bonaventure, *Major Life of St. Francis*, Ch. 13, 3

As you read this account of St. Francis, what lines or phrases especially touched your heart? What might these words about Francis inspire you to seek from the Lord? You may want to pray that you would come to have a deeper longing, a new fervor for Christ that raises you up to God and allows you to become more Christ-like. Your prayer might be that you could see how lovingly and graciously Christ looks upon you, so that you would grow more confident in His loving care.

This reading, though, reveals another prayer that we can find beneficial: The prayer that your life be united to Christ, and that any wounds, past or present, that you are carrying in your own heart, or mind, physical body or emotional being, be united to the holy wounds of Our Lord. Pray that your own bearing of any pain or hurt would lead to the comfort of knowing Christ more intimately. It takes great love to know Christ in this way, to bear with Him the wounds we carry. For we eventually realize that they are His wounds first. He knows them all and willingly received them for love of us. We can, in fact, take our wounds into His own, since we are reminded in 2 Corinthians 1:5, *"as Christ's sufferings overflow to us."*

But when we unite our places of pain to Christ, there is comfort and purpose. And when we offer them to the Lord for His holy work, there is healing. Prayerfully discern what places within yourself need to be united to Christ, and pray for the healing you need. Pray especially for the comfort of knowing Christ more intimately through this need. And may you be healed in every way as you make this walk with St. Francis.

Day 1: The Stigmata of St. Francis

*Blessed be the God and Father of our Lord Jesus Christ,
the Father of compassion and God of all cencouragement,
who encourages us in all our affliction, so that we may be able
to encourage those who are in any affliction, with the
encouragement with which we ourselves are encouraged by God.*
2 Corinthians 1:3-4

**Lord, let my desire be always to grow more and more
in Your image of love –
Your love that gives so purely and completely of itself.
I cannot do this without Your help.
I cannot love so deeply without Your love within me.
Please heal, restore, and make me new
in Your healing love.
Amen**

Days 2 – 5
For Our Love of God

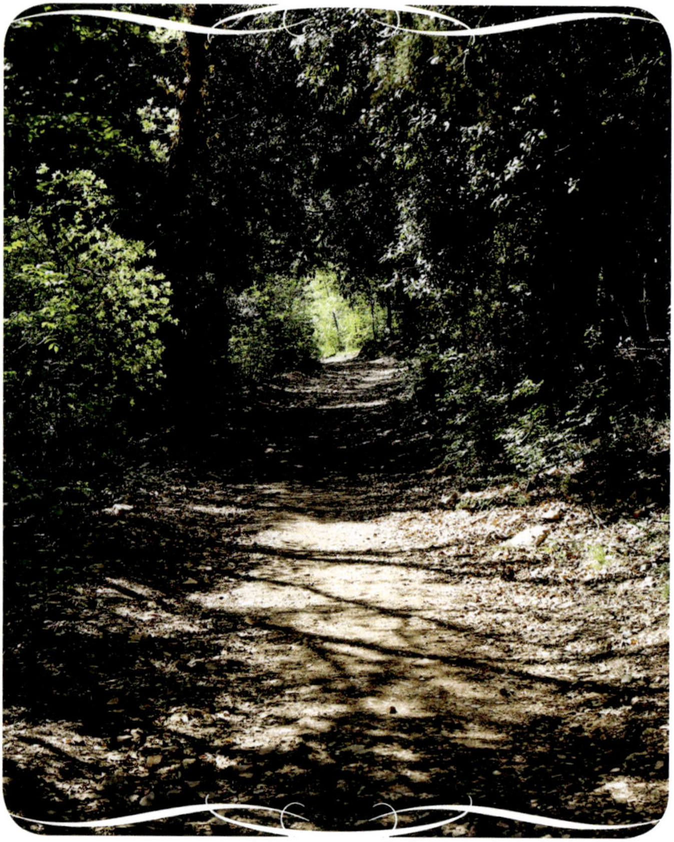

Day 2
Seeking Solitude

St. Francis never failed to keep himself occupied doing good; like the angels Jacob saw on the ladder (Gen. 28:12), he was always busy, either raising his heart to God in prayer, or descending to his neighbor. He had learned how to distribute the time in which he could gain merit wisely, devoting part of it to his neighbor by doing good, and part to the restful ecstasy of contemplation. According to the demands of time or circumstances he would devote himself wholly to the salvation of his neighbor, but when he was finished, he would escape from the distracting crowds and go into solitude in search of peace. There he was free to attend exclusively to God and he would cleanse any stain he had contracted while living in the midst of the world.

St. Bonaventure, *Major Life of St. Francis*, Ch. 13, 1

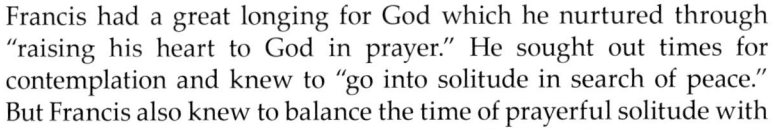

Francis had a great longing for God which he nurtured through "raising his heart to God in prayer." He sought out times for contemplation and knew to "go into solitude in search of peace." But Francis also knew to balance the time of prayerful solitude with another necessity – serving his neighbor. He knew how to use both as a way to give glory to God, and each way helped him to be more effective in the other.

Francis carried his 'fruits of contemplation' into his time of service to others. And his service to others helped Francis see and appreciate the great love and constant willingness in Christ's heart to serve all of humanity.

Prayerfully use your day to seek for places of solitude, and restore your peace in Christ's presence. Scripture tells us to *"Seek and you will find."* We may not always find a great space of time for this solitude, but we can better use those small moments of waiting in a line, or waiting between appointments, or those spaces of idle time we have between daily responsibilities. We can always balance our busy schedules with a word of prayer and taking a moment to refocus our thoughts toward God. I am frequently surprised when people tell me they often go through an entire day without being aware of God's presence. Since God is always with us, the 'absence of God' we feel may be a change we can make in ourselves. We may simply need to remind ourselves often of His love and faithful presence that never leaves or forsakes us.

Seek and you will find. I believe that when God sees our heart truly seeking Him, opportunities *will* open up for finding the solitude and strength we need in the Lord. Let us be more aware - and grateful - for His loving presence in our lives.

Ask, and it will be given you, seek, and you will find;
knock, and the door will be opened to you. For everyone who asks,
receives; and the one who seeks finds; and to the one who knocks,
the door will be opened.
Matthew 7: 7-8

Thank You, Lord, for moments of solitude
when I cannot find hours of it.
Thank You for providing Your presence
even if I cannot feel it as I go throughout my day.
Thank You for faithfully helping and providing
what I truly need. Today, Lord,
I will seek being with You with all my heart.
Amen

Day 3
The Beauty of God

Francis sought occasion to love God in everything. He delighted in all the works of God's hands and from the vision of joy on earth his mind soared aloft to the life-giving source and cause of all. In everything beautiful, he saw him who is beauty itself, and he followed his Beloved everywhere by his likeness imprinted on creation; of all creation he made a ladder by which he might mount up and embrace Him who is all-desirable. By the power of his extraordinary faith he tasted the Goodness which is the source of all in each and every created thing, as in so many rivulets. He seemed to perceive a divine harmony in the interplay of powers and faculties given by God to his creatures and like the prophet David he exhorted them all to praise God.

St. Bonaventure, *Major Life of St. Francis*, Ch. 9, 1

We have read here that Francis "sought occasion to love God in everything." The text mentions specifically that Francis saw the beauty of God's likeness "imprinted on creation."

We can all appreciate this beauty when we see a rainbow, or a magnificent mountain. But another 'beauty' we can delight in is God's work *within*. In addition to what we see all around us in a physical sense, there is also the beauty of God working all things together for good, the beauty of God's faithfulness, love, and constancy. There is the beauty of God's ways being deeper, wiser, and purer than our own. Francis saw these things, too, as the work of God's hands.

When we read that Francis "sought occasion to love God in

everything", we can be assured that he also sought occasion to love God in all circumstances, all encounters, all times of the day regardless of the situation.

Use this day to practice loving God and delighting in His wonderful works. Is there a situation in your life that repeatedly prompts you to dwell on the negative, the anxiousness, fear or dread of something? Make a determined effort to give God your thanks. Let your thoughts begin to dwell on the beauty of God working behind and within the situation. Remind yourself as often as the negative thoughts arise, that God's love is greater than any fear. God's presence is greater than any problem. God's authority is greater than any other controlling pressure. Think on these things, and replace any fears and complaints with faith, hope, and love, which always reflect God's beauty.

---

*Finally, brothers, whatever is true,
whatever is honorable, whatever is just, whatever is pure,
whatever is lovely, whatever is gracious, if there is any
excellence, if there is anything worthy of praise,
think about these things.*
Philippians 4:8

**My thoughts, Lord, are on You today.
I will try to keep them focused, please help me.
I will try to keep them filled with faith, please inspire me.
I will try to keep them ever aware of Your beauty
everywhere around me.
Please show me how to love You in everything.
Amen**

Day 4
The Worth of Divine Love

No human tongue could describe the passionate love with which Francis burned for Christ, his Spouse; he seemed to be completely absorbed by the fire of divine love like a glowing coal. The moment he heard the love of God being mentioned, he was aroused immediately and so deeply moved and inflamed that it seemed as if the deepest chord in his heart had been plucked by the words. He used to say that to offer the love of God in exchange for alms was generosity worthy of a nobleman and that anyone who thought less of it than money was a fool. The incalculable worth of divine love was the only thing that could win the kingdom of heaven. He used to say, "Greatly to be loved is His love, who loved us so greatly."

St. Bonaventure, *Major Life of St. Francis*, Ch. 9, 1

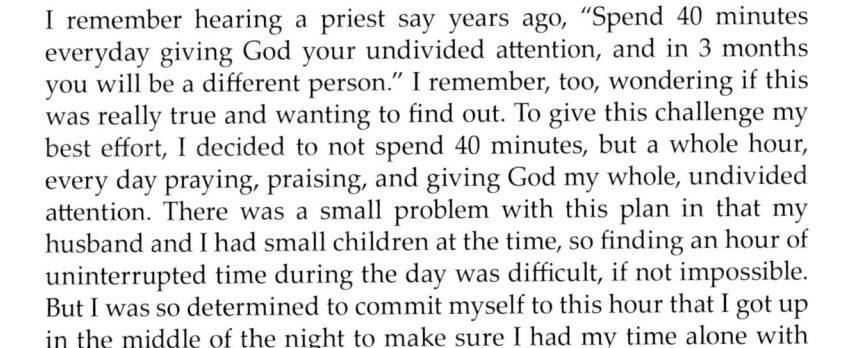

I remember hearing a priest say years ago, "Spend 40 minutes everyday giving God your undivided attention, and in 3 months you will be a different person." I remember, too, wondering if this was really true and wanting to find out. To give this challenge my best effort, I decided to not spend 40 minutes, but a whole hour, every day praying, praising, and giving God my whole, undivided attention. There was a small problem with this plan in that my husband and I had small children at the time, so finding an hour of uninterrupted time during the day was difficult, if not impossible. But I was so determined to commit myself to this hour that I got up in the middle of the night to make sure I had my time alone with God.

The priest was right! My life was changed. Even though I had always felt close to God and spent time in prayer, this very focused and attentive time began to feel like a complete emersion in God's love. It was transforming, and worth far more than anything I could have imagined. St. Francis knew *the incalculable worth of divine love*. And how valuable it is to realize that God wants *all of us* to know His love and to share it with others. Today bring yourself consciously, whole-heartedly, and gratefully, into the presence of Divine Love. You might even try doing this for a whole hour, and then you may want to continue it every day.

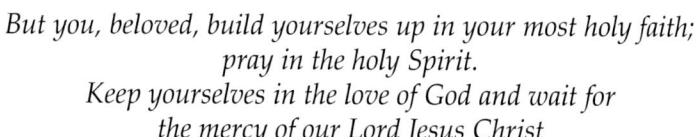

But you, beloved, build yourselves up in your most holy faith;
pray in the holy Spirit.
Keep yourselves in the love of God and wait for
the mercy of our Lord Jesus Christ
that leads to eternal life.
Jude 20-21

Lord, draw me more and more into the depths of Your love.
Let me have even a small glimpse of that love
which filled St. Francis and caused his heart to be
inflamed with love for You. Let me be made new by
Your love and grace – You who make all things new.
Amen

Day 5
Faithful Service

He withdrew from the busy life of his trade and begged God in his goodness to show him what he should do. He prayed constantly until he was consumed with a passionate longing for God and was ready to give up the whole world in his desire for his heavenly home and think nothing of it. He realized that he had discovered the treasure hidden in the field and like the wise trader in the Gospel he could think of nothing but how he might sell all that he had and buy the pearl he had found. He still did not know how to go about it, but at the same time he was forced to conclude that a spiritual venture could only begin by rejecting the world and that victory over himself would mark the beginning of his service of Christ.

St. Bonaventure, *Major Life of St. Francis*, Ch. 1, 4

How many times, I wonder, have people who accomplished great things, like St. Francis, began that venture while they "still did not know how to go about it"? It reminds us, again, that it is God who truly accomplishes any good that we do. Our part in this accomplishment is more about being emptied of self so that God can move in us and through us. Our part is learning to cooperate with the Lord's leading. Francis seemed to know that this cooperation would begin by rejecting worldly ways and overcoming his own ways. Francis began with what little he knew to do and he depended on God. It makes me wonder how many things might God be able to do through our lives if we would just do the same – faithfully follow the Lord in place of worldly desires and intentions, strive to overcome some interior self-centeredness in the moment we are in, and truly depend on God for the help we need.

It could be that God's will for each of us involves accomplishing great things, but we fail to see how very small things that *we do faithfully,* allow those great things to happen. Pay attention to your faithful service to God, especially in the very small things you have to do today.

The person who is trustworthy in very small matters is also trustworthy in great ones; and the person who is dishonest in very small matters is also dishonest in great ones.
Luke 16:10

**Lord, help me to follow the faithful guidance
You provide for me today.
I do not have to know how to go about
all that is in Your plan for me, but only be faithful
to You and Your holy way in the moment that is before me.
I thank You that my small steps of faithfulness can lead
to great steps in Your hands. I trust in You.
Amen**

Days 6 – 9
For Love of Poverty

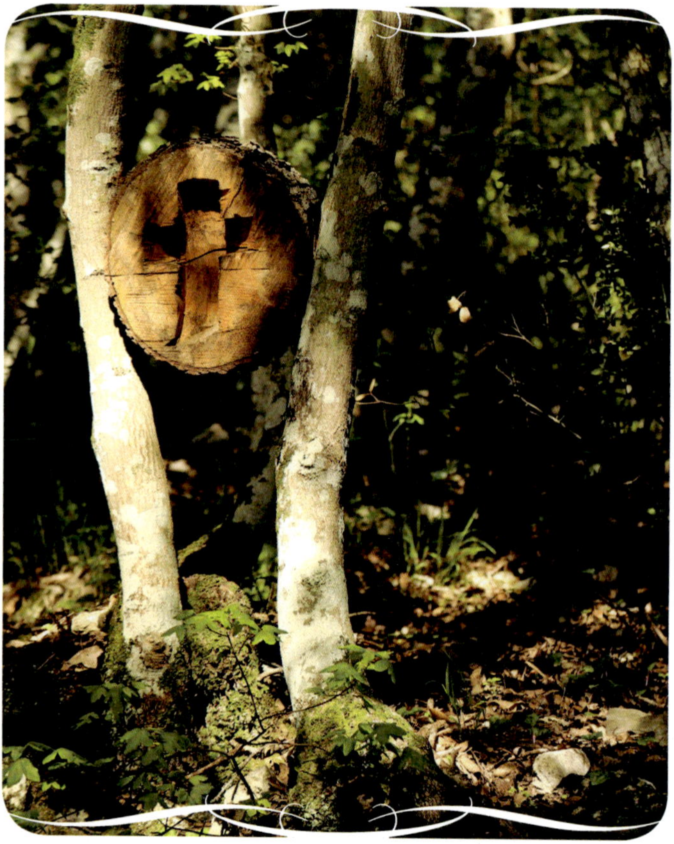

Day 6
Clearing Away Obstacles

The brothers were able to rejoice so truly in poverty because they did not desire riches and despised all passing things such as are pursued by those who love this world. Especially money they trampled underfoot; and following the teaching and example of Saint Francis, they considered gold as having the same weight and worth as the dung of an ass. They rejoiced continually in the Lord because, in themselves, and between each other, there existed nothing to disturb them. The more they were separated from the world, the closer became their union with God. They followed the narrow way of the cross and the path of righteousness; and they cleared away all obstacles from the way of penitence and the observance of the Gospel in order to make the path smooth and safe for those who were to come after them.

Legend of the Three Companions, 45

I find this reading very interesting, especially that they "rejoiced continually in the Lord…" and "the more they were separated from the world, the closer became their union with God."

We always seem to be working on our own personal "separation from the world" which will be varied from one person to the next. Francis and his brothers, Clare and her sisters, showed us the most complete way to live this. I cannot imagine what foundation of poverty would have been laid for us if those first followers had not been so careful to "make the path smooth and safe for those who were to come after them." And this, of course, is another reason we all have to bear in mind how we are living this. Those who follow Francis are continually repairing and re-laying this foundation for others to see.

Something else to bear in mind from this story is the connection that is made between the friars' "separation from the world" and the "closer became their union with God". Have you ever thought that living without a sense of the Lord's peace and well-being in life might very well be an indication that worldly attachments are taking priority over God's rightful place? Prayerfully consider what the Holy Spirit is saying to you regarding this reading. If you sense a wrong attachment to something in your life, give it in prayer to the Lord. We can usually discover how attached we are by the anxiety we feel over - even the thought of - losing it. If there is a wrong attachment to something worldly, reestablish your love for the Lord, and ask for His help and grace to live more fully in Him. Begin with establishing your own, deeply rooted and personal dwelling in Christ, then all that is beneath Him can take their rightful place in your life.

If then you were raised with Christ, seek what is above,
where Christ is seated at the right hand of God.
Think of what is above,
not of what is on earth.
Colossians 3:1-2

Lord, I give you today all places of my heart and mind
that are obstacles to my union with You.
Those places that I am not aware of, I pray You
would expose to the light of Your holy love,
and I ask You to help me live with increasing
faith and love for You and Your kingdom.
Amen

Day 7
Poverty's Surrender

In the early days of the Order, while he was traveling with a friar who was one of the first twelve, he used to greet men and women along the road and in the fields, saying, 'The Lord give you peace.' And because people had never heard such a greeting from any Religious, they were very startled. Indeed, some said indignantly, 'What do you mean by this greeting of yours?' As a result the friar became embarrassed, and said to blessed Francis, 'Allow me to use some other greeting.' But the holy Father said, "Let them chatter, for they do not understand the ways of God. Don't feel ashamed because of this, for one day the nobles and princes of this world will respect you and other friars for this greeting. For it is no marvel if the Lord should desire to have a new little flock, whose speech and way of life are unlike those of all its predecessors, and which is content to possess him alone, the Most High and most glorious."

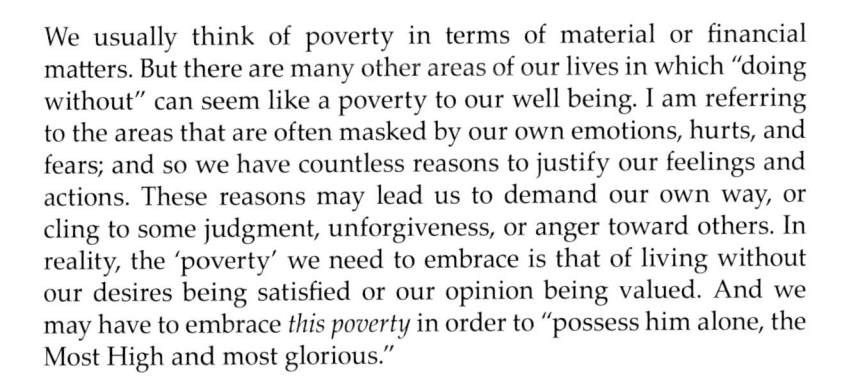

Mirror of Perfection, 26

We usually think of poverty in terms of material or financial matters. But there are many other areas of our lives in which "doing without" can seem like a poverty to our well being. I am referring to the areas that are often masked by our own emotions, hurts, and fears; and so we have countless reasons to justify our feelings and actions. These reasons may lead us to demand our own way, or cling to some judgment, unforgiveness, or anger toward others. In reality, the 'poverty' we need to embrace is that of living without our desires being satisfied or our opinion being valued. And we may have to embrace *this poverty* in order to "possess him alone, the Most High and most glorious."

I will offer an example from my own life: Because of a physical need I have, I can frequently experience discomfort or pain and, of course, the discouragement that often accompanies a chronic physical problem. One day in prayer, (and I had just been reading about St. Francis' love of poverty), by the grace of God, I began to see my health as a kind of 'poverty' that I could accept and use to deepen my trust in God. I saw this act as doing without my will in order to fully embrace God's plan for me. How often are we reminded that God says to us, *"My thoughts are not your thoughts, nor are your ways My ways."?* (Isaiah 55:8) I prayed a sincere prayer of surrender, which I had done I thought many times before, but this time a true "healing" took place in my heart. I was able to see a deeper way of raising myself up to God specifically through this 'poverty' of my health. Sometimes the poverty we need to accept is that of living without seeing our will answered and trusting, instead, our Father's love and authority to choose what is best for us. Would not such a faithful surrender in our heart allow us to receive God and His ways more fully? And receiving God would then allow us to receive the *peace of God* in our hearts that we could offer sincerly to others. Prayerfully examine whether there is a 'possession' you may be clinging to (material, emotional, intellectual, or physical), and seek God's will for any 'poverty' you should accept in its place in order to 'possess him alone.'

Indeed I shall continue to rejoice, for I know that this will result in deliverance for me through your prayers and support from the Spirit of Jesus Christ. My eager expectation and hope is that I shall not be put to shame in any way, but that with all boldness, now as always, Christ will be magnified in my body, whether by life or by death. For to me life is Christ, and death is gain.
Philippians 1: 19-21

**Lord, let me grow continually in Your thoughts and Your ways. Let me not be enticed by the traps of this world which are alluring but empty. Let me see clearly those things I need to surrender in order to continue on the way that leads to You.
Amen**

Day 8
The Riches of Poverty

St. Francis often used to say to the friars: "I recommend these three words to you, namely, holy *simplicity* against an inordinate appetite for knowledge, *prayer* which the devil always tries to set aside by many exterior occupations and worries, and the *love of poverty*, not just poverty itself, the spouse of the Lord Jesus Christ and my spouse, but love and zeal for it.

Little Flowers of St. Francis, 13

St. Francis is telling his friars that there is such great richness in choosing poverty that they should have great love and zeal for it. That thought alone sounds so foreign to us in the culture we live in today. It seems that the values of simplicity and poverty have been lost to us. Our hearts have been hardened and our eyes blinded by the 'treasures' we have today – especially the treasures of convenience, instant gratification, and entertainment. So much is available to us, almost as soon as we want it. In today's culture, how well are we learning to wait for something, work hard and long for something, or do completely without something?

Francis wants to show us the way to God's greater "riches". *Simplicity* helps us keep things in proper perspective and provides a trustworthy 'backdrop' for exposing self-centered desires. *Prayer* draws us into a deeper union with God, and puts us in that humble position where God's helping grace can flow into our lives. *Poverty*, Francis reminds us, is the spouse of the Lord Jesus Christ because our Lord left His heavenly kingdom for love of us and *"gave himself for us to deliver us"* (Titus 2:14), *"emptied himself, taking the form of a slave"* (Philippians 2:7), and chose to *"do nothing on my own authority"* but spoke only *as the Father* taught him (John 8:28). In every way, Christ chose the poverty of denying Himself – of His will, His power, and His authority – for love of the Father and love of humanity.

And so, for Francis, there was love and zeal in surrendering his will, in trusting God's power, and in relying completely upon God's authority. If Christ did so, what could be better or 'richer' for us than to follow in the same way?

How do we find the richness that Francis was talking about and Christ was showing us, if we do not take some steps each day to live more in simplicity, prayer, and love of poverty? How might you better live these 3 recommendations that Francis gave to his friars? Make a list of the steps you could take today.

In the same way, everyone of you who does not renounce all his possessions cannot be my disciple.
Luke 14:33

**Today, Lord, I give You all that I have,
to use according to Your holy will.
Help me to release to You my desires,
my attachments, and all my will.
Help me to live in the simplicity,
prayer, and poverty, that allows You
to make of my life the gift You
have always intended it to be.
Amen**

Day 9
A Humble Dwelling Place for God

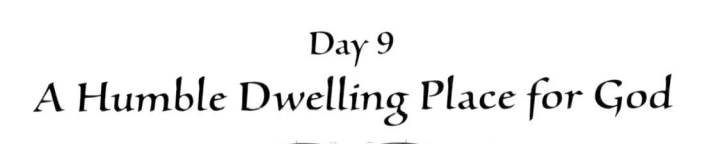

In that love which is God, I entreat all my friars, ministers and subjects, to put away every attachment, all care and solicitude, and serve, love, honor, and adore our Lord and God with a pure heart and mind; this is what he seeks above all else. We should make a dwelling-place within ourselves where he can stay, he who is the Lord God almighty, Father, Son, and Holy Spirit.

The Rule of 1221, Ch. 22

We can usually see how earthly attachments may interfere with our love and service to God. But St. Francis mentions here that there should be a putting away of "all care and solicitude" as well. That is not so easily done for some of us. How do we put away anxieties, concerns, and worries that interfere with our love of God, even if we want to?

I think, like any attachment we have, in order to give it up, it helps to have a worthy replacement. St. Francis exhorts his followers to 'love poverty' so that one can embrace Christ fully. He wants our hearts and minds to be "pure" because this is what the Lord "seeks above all else." Let us remember, then, *why* the Lord would seek this purity in us.

The Lord's love is completely other-focused so His desire for us is always for our good. He desires purity in us so that He can have a dwelling place. The Lord God almighty, Father, Son, and Holy Spirit wants to reside and dwell intimately within us. What could we want more than this? And if the *Lord wants this*, what anxieties or concerns could be so great as to keep us distracted from His gracious request?

In yesterday's reading Francis was recommending *"prayer, which the devil always tries to set aside by many exterior occupations and worries."* Have you noticed how often we can be distracted from prayer and thinking about the Lord because our minds are caught up in the problems of the day? If we only knew how much it blesses and glorifies God to see that we trust Him with our welfare at all times. If we only knew how much it blesses and glorifies God to see that we have great faith in what He can do. If we only knew how much it glorifies God – and defeats the devil – we would pray with greater hope and be more determined to deny our minds and hearts of worry. Today, create this dwelling-place within yourself through prayerful faith and hope. And do not let any anxious thoughts distract you with problems that the Lord already knows how to solve.

*May the God of hope fill you with
all joy and peace in believing,
so that you may abound in hope
by the power of the holy Spirit.*
Romans 15:13

Lord, I want to create a dwelling place for You in my heart.
Help me to serve, love, and adore You
with a pure heart and mind
so that You may come and reside fully within me.
I know I can trust You with every need and longing,
which I give to You now.
And in place of fears and worries,
I give You thanks, my Lord.
Amen.

Days 10 – 13
For Love of the Cross

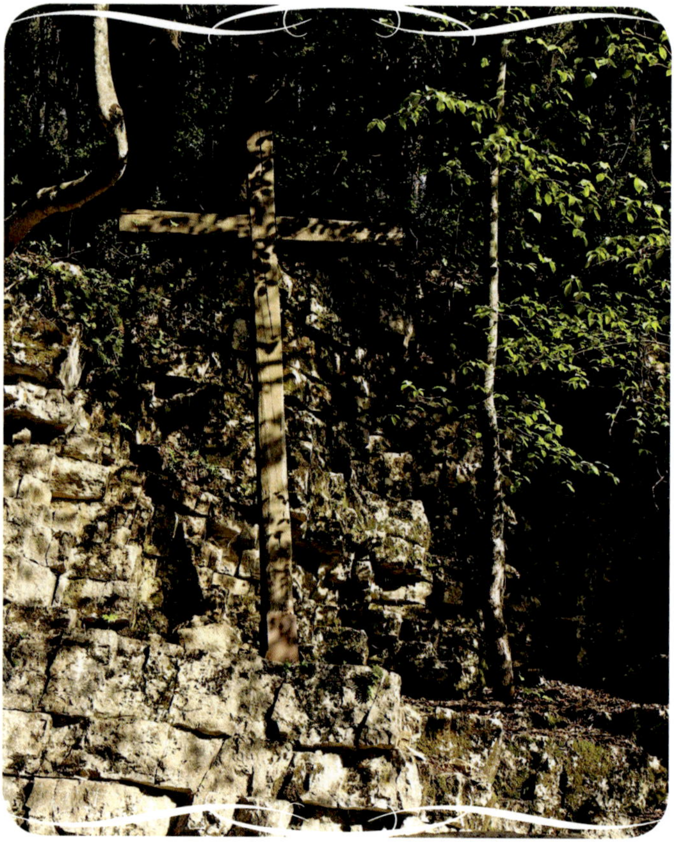

Day 10
Sharing the Needs of Others

In those days, Blessed Francis was living at the hermitage of St. Eleutherius, not far from Contigliano, in the district of Rieti. Since he was wearing but one tunic and it was extremely cold, he was obliged to line the inside of it; so did his companion. His body felt some relief from this. A short time after, as he had just finished his prayer, overjoyed, he said to his companion: "I must be a model and an example to all the brothers. Therefore, although my body needs a lined tunic, I must think of my brothers who are experiencing the same need and who do not have or cannot procure for themselves a like tunic. I must therefore put myself in their place and share their privations, so that they may endure them patiently because they see the way I live."

Legend of Perugia, 85

Francis has something very important to teach us in this story. He wants to put himself in the place of those brothers who have less than he has "and share their privations." He states that he should do this because he can show them by example how to bear this with patience and trust in the Lord. But there is more to this example. Francis knew what a gift it was to share in someone else's suffering because he knew, and deeply loved, that Christ came to share in our suffering.

I frequently tell people in spiritual direction that if they are suffering a particular illness, or separation from loved ones, or some other need they are enduring at the time, to pray especially for all the other people who are going through that same need, but do not have the faith to turn to God. Sometimes the only difference between our afflictions and what afflicts others, is that we have faith to sustain us. We know and trust in the Lord who *"heals the brokenhearted and binds up their wounds."* (Psalm 147:3) We know how to turn to God and *"receive mercy and to find grace for timely help."* (Hebrews 4:16)

And just as Christ came to share in our humanity so that we could share in his divinity, we are given a great gift by participating with Christ in this cross-carrying act of love. Our prayers are taking that particular need and offering it to God for others who are struggling with that same need but will not pray. We are offering it to God *for* them. So, offer your sufferings, your hardships, and even your temporary disappointments to the Lord, and pray for all those who are suffering in like manner but will not lift it up to God. You have no idea how your prayers for someone else can 'open the doors' for God's grace to move in their hearts and make a difference. Christ, who does so much for us in our pain, will lovingly accept your prayers and offerings for others.

For as Christ's sufferings overflow to us,
so through Christ does our encouragement also overflow.
2 Corinthians 1:5

Lord, make me a better instrument of
Your love and prayerful sacrifice.
Let me not waste an opportunity to make a
'gift' to You of some discomfort or hardship I bear.
So many are going through the same suffering
without knowing that You love and care for them.
Help me to love as You love, and to offer myself
as You so willingly did for me.
Amen

Day 11
Bearing Sister-Suffering

With Christ for his leader, he proposed to achieve great victories, and even as his limbs bordered on collapse, he hoped to triumph over his enemy the Devil once again, because he was fervent and courageous in spirit. Merit, as we know, is crowned by patient endurance, and so, as Christ's poor, worthless servant, Francis began to suffer from a variety of illnesses, that his treasure of glory might be increased. His suffering was so great that there was not a single part of him which did not have its share of agony; he had no flesh left and his skin seemed to cling to his bones. He was hemmed in with agonizing pain, but he called his cruel sufferings his sisters, not his pains. He bore them joyfully and praised God, thanking him for everything; the humble and happy way he could rejoice in his suffering reminded the friars who were looking after him of St. Paul, while the courage of his steadfast spirit made him seem like a second Job.

Bonaventure, *Minor Life of St. Francis*, Ch. 7, 2

We might certainly, and rightfully, ask why St. Francis gave thanks to God in his pain and referred to his sufferings as 'his sisters'. Let us remember that for Francis, the spiritual world was just as present and perceptible as the physical. He lived, in a sense, in both worlds. But once you see God's Kingdom in the splendor and beauty of the spiritual realm, the physical world is only a means to get there, and Francis wanted to use his physical encounters and experiences to their fullest advantage. He knew that his 'sisters', as he called them, were helping him grow more into the image of Christ. And he knew, as well, Paul's words to the Colossians (1:24), *"I rejoice in my sufferings for your sake, and in my flesh I am filling up what is lacking in the afflictions of Christ on behalf of his body, which is the church... ."*

He looked at this life always through the lens of eternal truth, where: love allows only what can be used for good, and suffering has a purpose that far outweighs the pain, and the sorrows of this life are purifying and end in joy because death to this world brings everlasting life.

We may not see the spiritual realm as Francis did, but we can be encouraged through his words and example. And maybe, as in poverty, the more we choose to live following his footsteps, the more our eyes will be opened and our hearts fashioned to the truths he saw so clearly.

---

*It is the Spirit itself bears witness with our spirit
that we are children of God,
and if children, then heirs, heirs of God
and joint heirs with Christ,
if only we suffer with him so
that we may also be glorified with him.*
Romans 8:16-17

**Lord, open my eyes to the truth and the joys
of Your kingdom. Help me to be like St. Francis in
bringing Your kingdom of heaven to earth,
so that others can see that Your love reigns supreme.
Allow me to see through the 'lens of eternal truth'
and to live in this world so as to be ready
for the world to come.
Amen**

Day 12
Practicing Perfect Joy

One winter day St. Francis was coming to St. Mary of the Angels from Perugia with Brother Leo, and the bitter cold made them suffer keenly. St. Francis called to Brother Leo, who was walking a bit ahead of him, and he said: "Brother Leo, even if the Friars Minor in every country give a great example of holiness and integrity and good edification, nevertheless write down and note carefully that perfect joy is not in that." …And going on a bit, St. Francis cried out again…"Brother Leo, if a Friar Minor knew all languages and all sciences and Scripture, if he also knew how to prophesy and to reveal not only the future but also the secrets of the consciences and minds of others, write down and note carefully that perfect joy is not in that."…And going on a bit farther, St. Francis called again… "Brother Leo, even if a Friar Minor could preach so well that he should convert all infidels to the faith of Christ, write that perfect joy is not there."…Brother Leo in great amazement asked him: "Father, I beg you in God's name to tell me where perfect joy is." And St. Francis replied: "When we come to St. Mary of the Angels, soaked by the rain and frozen by the cold, …and we ring at the gate …and brother porter comes and says angrily: 'Who are you?' And we say: 'We are two of your brothers.' And he contradicts us, saying: 'You are not telling the truth.' …And if we continue to knock, and the porter comes out in anger, and drives us away with curses and hard blows …and if we bear it patiently and take the insults with joy and love in our hearts, …if we endure all those evils and insults and blows with joy and patience, reflecting that we must accept and bear the sufferings of the Blessed Christ patiently for love of Him, oh, Brother Leo, write: that is perfect joy! …Above all the graces and gifts of the Holy Spirit which Christ gives to His friends is that of conquering oneself and willingly enduring sufferings, insults, humiliations, and hardships for the love of Christ.

Little Flowers of St. Francis, 8

This is a wonderful story, and well worth reading in its entirety. But even in this condensed version we are left with a lot to ponder. Francis is explaining to Brother Leo that perfect joy does not come from those things we normally enjoy and desire, but in that which helps us conquer ourselves. Whatever enables us to overcome self-centered tendencies and makes us more Christ-like, are the real joys we should delight in. Let us look specifically at 3 *'joys'* we might find in Francis' words. First is the joy that Francis states so clearly: We should want to *conquer the self-absorption* we naturally have, and be glad to acquire, instead, other-focused love, which is the nature of God. Second is the joy of *enduring suffering for love of Christ*, since Christ chose to endure suffering for love of us. Do we really grasp what Christ accomplished for us in this pure and selfless act of love? The mere thought should fill us with joy. Our own suffering, then, in patience and peace will express our deep trust and gratitude to Him. And third is the joy of *comforting* Christ with this only thing that is ours – our tribulations and afflictions. How does this bring comfort to Christ? It is because Christ sees that His selfless act of suffering for us was not in vain. His love has been received, and now returned, through our own act of surrendered imitation – rejoicing in God throughout all life circumstances. Practice perfect joy today in all your situations.

Beloved, do not be surprised that a trial by fire is occurring among you, as if something strange were happening to you. But rejoice to the extent that you share in the sufferings of Christ, so that when his glory is revealed you may also rejoice exultantly.
1 Peter 4:12-13

Your joy, Lord, is a great gift. Let me learn to rejoice in Your presence and live the words we read in Nehemiah: *Do not be grieved, for the joy of the Lord is your strength.* **(8:10) Amen**

Day 13
Directing Our Efforts to God

It was only right that St. Francis should be decorated with this extraordinary privilege; all his efforts, whether they were known to others or made in secret, were directed towards our Lord's Cross. What was his extreme gentleness, his austerity, his deep humility, his ready obedience, his absolute poverty, his perfect chastity; what were his bitter contrition, his gift of tears, his heartfelt compassion, his ardent zeal, his longing for martyrdom, his unlimited charity; what were all the outstanding virtues which made him so like Christ, if not the signs of an ever increasing likeness to him and a preparation for the reception of his stigmata? The whole course of his life from the very beginning was marked with the glorious mysteries of Christ's Cross. Eventually, at the site of the majestic Seraph and of the abjection of Christ crucified, he was completely changed into the likeness of what he saw by a transforming fire of divine origin. For this we have the testimony of those who saw the stigmata and felt and kissed them; they took an oath that this was true, asserting that they had seen them with their own eyes and so made their testimony more certain.

Bonaventure, *Minor Life of Saint Francis*, Ch 6, 9

As you read this account, I think it worthwhile to first notice what specific sentences touch your heart and your attention. You might even take a moment to do that before you read on.

For myself, I noticed that Francis' efforts were "directed towards our Lord's Cross." This made an impression on me because we are more often reminded that we each have our *own cross* to bear if we want to follow the Lord, as Christ said, *"Whoever wishes to come after me must deny himself, take up his cross, and follow me."* (Matthew 16:24)

But this thought that Francis directed all his efforts "towards our Lord's Cross" reminds us that ultimately, every trial or suffering or 'cross' we carry is first and foremost a participation with Christ in what He so graciously carried for us. Not only are we not alone in carrying a burden or hardship, but before we ever knew our cross was coming, Christ knew it, accepted it, and in a sense, 'carried it' for us. Now it is for us to take it up and bear it *with Christ*, but always remembering that His triumphant grace and resurrection power are with us in transforming ways. This story reminds us that the burden in Francis' heart was directed to *the Lord's suffering* more than his own. This, too, is important to apply to ourselves since we always seem able to bear *more* when love compels us to bear our suffering for someone else.

This story makes me think that St. Francis saw every 'cross' in his life as one that was completely yoked to the Cross of Christ, and consequently, the Lord was able to make Francis' yoke easier, and his burden bearable – to the glory of God! Is there a 'cross' in your life that needs to be securely yoked to Christ?

Come to me, all who labor and are burdened,
and I will give you rest.
Take my yoke upon you and learn from me,
for I am meek and humble of heart,
and you will find rest for you selves.
For my yoke is easy, and my burden is light.
Matthew 11:28-30

Lord, thank You for taking up my cross so that
I could be drawn to new life in You.
I ask You to help me, at each moment,
to trustingly follow You in
bearing all that I am called to bear,
all that I am meant to carry.
Let me direct all my efforts to Your Holy Cross,
and to find myself at Your side with
Your faithful yoke sustaining me.
Amen

Days 14 – 17
For Imitation of Christ

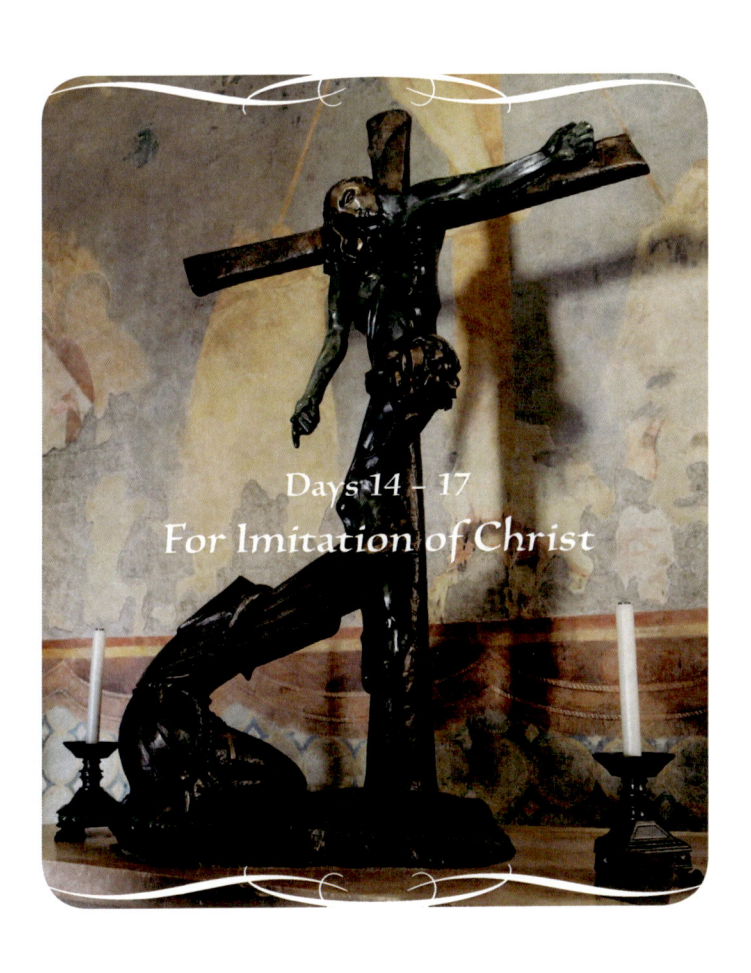

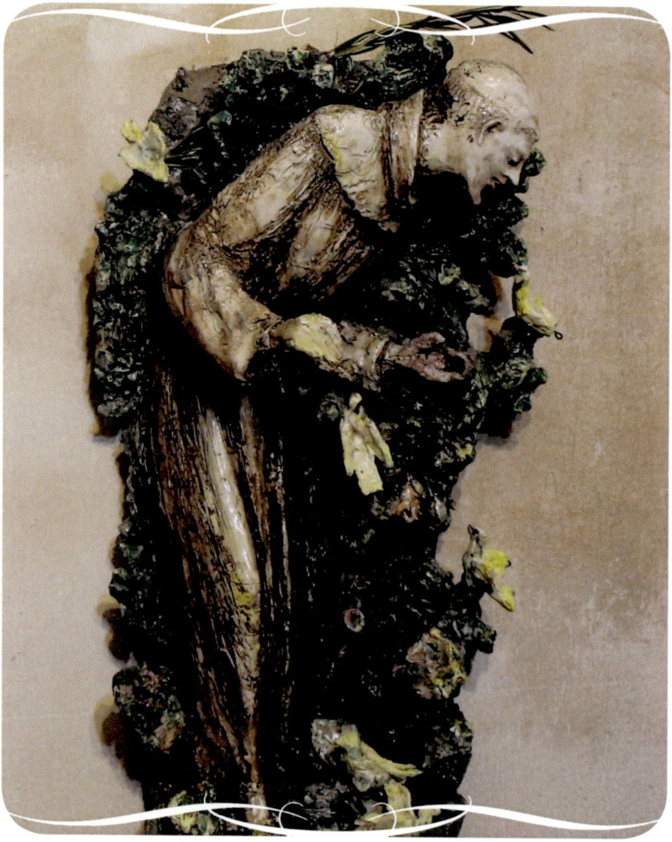

Day 14
Growing in Virtue

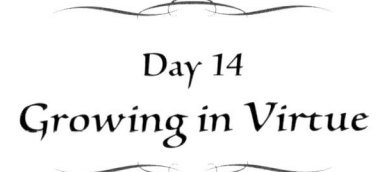

Hail, Queen Wisdom! The Lord save you,
with your sister, pure, holy Simplicity.
Lady Holy Poverty, God keep you,
with your sister, holy Humility,
Lady Holy Love, God keep you,
with your sister, holy Obedience.
All holy virtues, God keep you,
God, from whom you proceed and come.
In all the world there is not a man who can possess
any one of you without first dying to himself.
The man who practices one and does not offend
against the others possesses all;
the man who offends against one,
possesses none and violates all.
Each and every one of you puts vice and sin to shame.

from - *The Praises of the Virtues* - St. Francis of Assisi

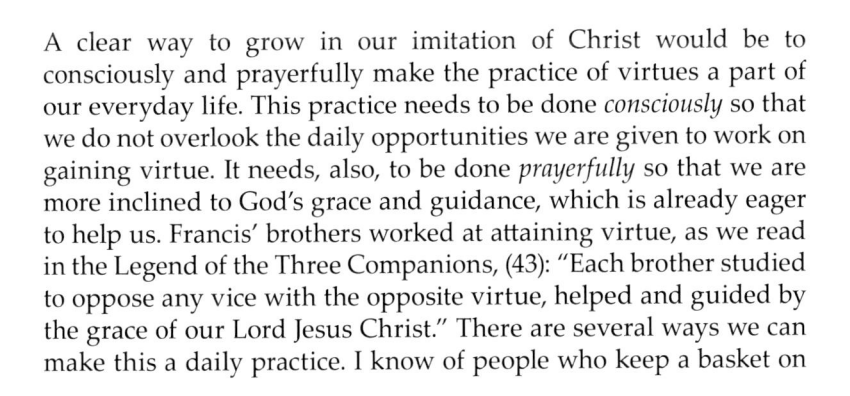

A clear way to grow in our imitation of Christ would be to consciously and prayerfully make the practice of virtues a part of our everyday life. This practice needs to be done *consciously* so that we do not overlook the daily opportunities we are given to work on gaining virtue. It needs, also, to be done *prayerfully* so that we are more inclined to God's grace and guidance, which is already eager to help us. Francis' brothers worked at attaining virtue, as we read in the Legend of the Three Companions, (43): "Each brother studied to oppose any vice with the opposite virtue, helped and guided by the grace of our Lord Jesus Christ." There are several ways we can make this a daily practice. I know of people who keep a basket on their table containing many small slips of paper, each of which has written on it one virtue. The virtue you pull out of the basket is the one you will practice that day or that week. As you pray the rosary, you could pray to grow in one virtue at each decade. Another way is to look through the readings at Sunday Mass. Which virtue would best help you live the message of the Gospel that week? Or, you could simply keep in mind the virtues most appropriate to your present circumstances. What does your situation today give you an opportunity to practice in your imitation of Christ? Is it patience, or mercy, or faith, or something else?

The Lord is always sending us encouragement, so keep in mind as you do this: God wants to help you and is delighted when we are trying to grow in those holy qualities that reflect the kingdom of God. Do not get discouraged if you seem to fail repeatedly. Perseverance, prayer, and the Lord's grace are powerfully present aids to help us. Finally, as we saw on Day 10, as you are trying to put a particular virtue into practice, especially when it is difficult, make your efforts to gain virtue an offering to God for someone else who needs, also, to grow in that same virtue. Begin today. I am sure St. Francis is prayerfully cheering you on.

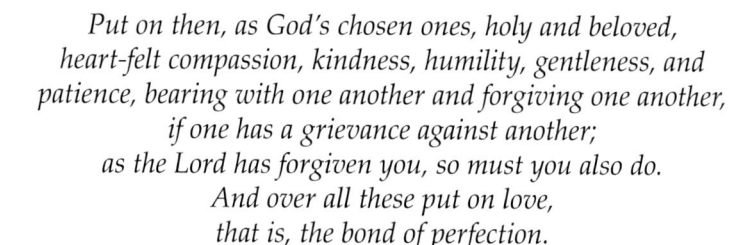

Put on then, as God's chosen ones, holy and beloved,
heart-felt compassion, kindness, humility, gentleness, and
patience, bearing with one another and forgiving one another,
if one has a grievance against another;
as the Lord has forgiven you, so must you also do.
And over all these put on love,
that is, the bond of perfection.
Colossians 3:12-14

Help me, Lord, to more deeply appreciate the gift you offer
to us – this gift to grow in Your holy image and likeness.
Each day I have the opportunity to grow in virtue,
and I pray for Your grace to let me not ignore my chance
to honor You and imitate Your goodness.
Amen

Day 15
Purity and Spiritual Joy

From the beginning of his conversion to the day of his death, blessed Francis had always been hard on his body. But his primary and main concern was always to possess and preserve spiritual joy within and without. He declared that if the servant of God strove to possess and preserve interior and external spiritual joy, which proceeds from purity of heart, the devils could do him no harm, but would be forced to admit: "Since this servant of God preserves his joy in tribulation as well as in prosperity, we can find no way to harm his soul."…

He also said: "I know that the devils envy me because of all the graces I have received from the goodness of the Lord. Since they cannot harm me directly, they try to do it in my companions. If they cannot strike either me or my companions, they withdraw full of confusion. Conversely, if I happen to be tempted and downcast, I need only contemplate the joy of a companion and I go from the temptation and despondency to interior joy."

Legend of Perugia, 97

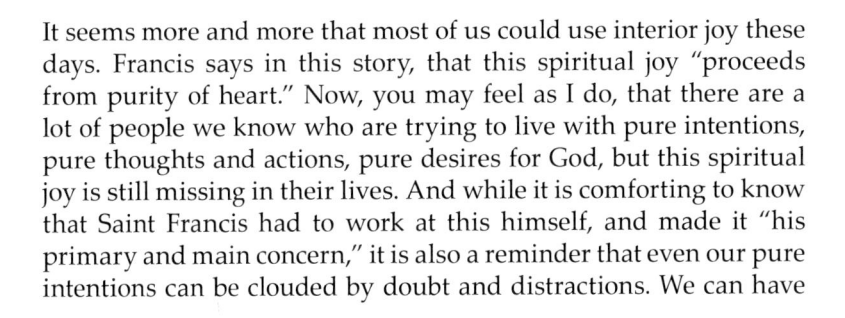

It seems more and more that most of us could use interior joy these days. Francis says in this story, that this spiritual joy "proceeds from purity of heart." Now, you may feel as I do, that there are a lot of people we know who are trying to live with pure intentions, pure thoughts and actions, pure desires for God, but this spiritual joy is still missing in their lives. And while it is comforting to know that Saint Francis had to work at this himself, and made it "his primary and main concern," it is also a reminder that even our pure intentions can be clouded by doubt and distractions. We can have pure desires, but still see fears or discouragement interfere.

The real message here, I think, is this: To preserve our interior and external spiritual joy, we have to be devoted to, focused on, and continually present to the *purity of God* – which never changes or diminishes, and always longs for us. That, for me, is where to find joy – it is in knowing how loving and good and present God is toward us. Then, the more we strive to be close to our Lord, as Francis did, the more our own heart will become pure from exposure to His holy light.

And, too, we are finding our joy in something that does not change with our circumstances. If we want to maintain this purity in ourselves, it is done by striving to live "with Him, in Him, and through Him" *Who is* truly pure of heart. And in that way we will possess our own interior and external spiritual joy. Let us praise and thank our Lord who wants purity and joy for us!

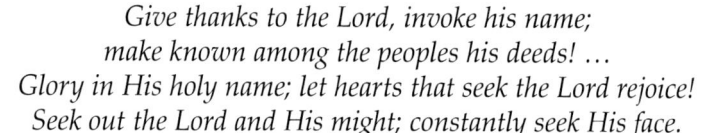

Give thanks to the Lord, invoke his name;
make known among the peoples his deeds! …
Glory in His holy name; let hearts that seek the Lord rejoice!
Seek out the Lord and His might; constantly seek His face.
Psalm 105: 1, 3-4

Lord, I do seek Your presence, and I rejoice that
You allow me to do so. I seek, too, the graces
I need to be pure of heart. May Your image of love
and faithfulness, purity and joy, peace and compassion
fill me and pour out of me to reach others with Your love.
Amen

Day 16
Intimacy with Christ

The memory of Christ Jesus crucified was ever present in the depths of his heart like a bundle of myrrh, and he longed to be wholly transformed into him by the fire of love. In his extraordinary devotion to Christ, he fasted every year for forty days, beginning at the Epiphany, the time when Christ himself lived in the desert. Then he would go to some lonely place and remain there shut up in his cell, taking as little food and drink as possible, as he spent all his time praying and praising God. He loved Christ so fervently and Christ returned his love so intimately that he seemed to have his Savior before his eyes continually, as he once privately admitted to his companions. He burned with love for the Sacrament of our Lord's Body with all his heart, and was lost in wonder at the thought of such condescending love, such loving condescension. He received Holy Communion often and so devoutly that he roused others to devotion too. The presence of the Immaculate Lamb used to take him out of himself, so that he was often lost in ecstasy.

Bonaventure, *Major Life of St. Francis*, Ch. 9, 2

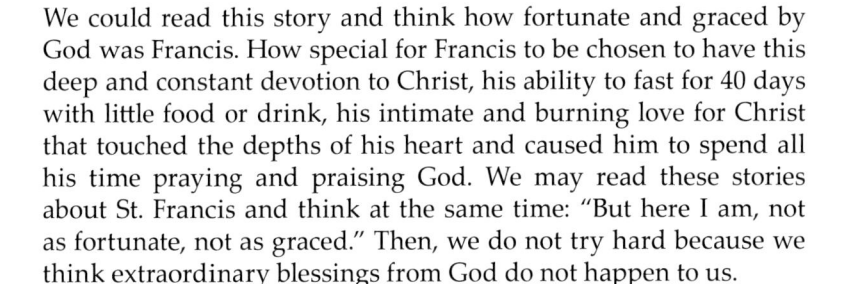

We could read this story and think how fortunate and graced by God was Francis. How special for Francis to be chosen to have this deep and constant devotion to Christ, his ability to fast for 40 days with little food or drink, his intimate and burning love for Christ that touched the depths of his heart and caused him to spend all his time praying and praising God. We may read these stories about St. Francis and think at the same time: "But here I am, not as fortunate, not as graced." Then, we do not try hard because we think extraordinary blessings from God do not happen to us.

Though we might be tempted to think that way, we must be careful to never overlook the *most extraordinary blessing* mentioned in this whole story, because it is a blessing *each of us* are offered from the Lord – the Sacrament of our Lord's Body.

We are able to receive, just as Francis did, the Immaculate Lamb – this 'holy and living sacrifice' – Christ's true presence in the Eucharist. Let us praise and thank Our Lord for this gift, as St. Francis did, and be continuously mindful that it will help us grow in our imitation of Christ. Francis' Letter to a General Chapter reminds us:

"Our whole being should be seized with fear, the whole world should tremble and heaven rejoice, when Christ the Son of the living God is present on the altar in the hands of the priest. What wonderful majesty! What stupendous condescension! O sublime humility! That the Lord of the whole universe, God and the Son of God, should humble himself like this and hide under the form of a little bread for our salvation. Look at God's condescension, my brothers, and pour out your hearts before him. Humble yourselves that you may be exalted by him. Keep nothing for yourselves, so that he who has given himself wholly to you may receive you wholly."

Jesus said the them, "I am the bread of life; whoever comes to me will never hunger, and whoever believes in me will never thirst...
For this is the will of my Father, that every one who sees the Son and believes in him may have eternal life, and I shall raise him [on] the last day."
John 6:35 + 40

My Lord and my God! You truly provide for my needs, even for those needs I take too lightly sometimes. Thank You for Your precious gift of the Eucharist. May I receive You with all gratitude and devotion for the help You give me to live in greater imitation of You.
Amen

Day 17
Living Our Blessing

The most holy Father had now been informed by the Holy Spirit as well as by the doctors that his death was near. Hitherto he had been lodged in the bishop's palace, but when he felt himself growing steadily worse and his bodily powers failing, he asked to be carried on a litter to S. Mary of the Porziuncula, so that his bodily life should draw to its close in the place where his spiritual life and light had come into being.

When the brethren who were carrying him arrived at the hospice standing by the road half-way between Assisi and S. Mary's, he asked the bearers to set the litter on the ground. And although his long-standing and severe disease of the eyes had almost deprived him of sight, he had the litter turned to face the city of Assisi. Raising himself a little, he blessed the city, saying "Lord, it is said that in former days this city was the haunt of wicked men. But now it is clear that of Thine infinite mercy and in Thine own time Thou hast been pleased to shower especial and abundant favors upon it. Of Thy goodness alone Thou hast chosen it for Thyself, that it may become the home and dwelling of those who know Thee in truth and glorify Thy holy Name, and spread abroad the fragrance of a good report, of holy life, of true doctrine, and of evangelical perfection to all Christian people. I therefore beseech Thee, O Lord Jesus Christ, Father of mercies, that Thou wilt not remember our ingratitude, but ever be mindful of Thine abundant compassion which Thou hast showed towards it, that it may ever be the home and dwelling-place of those who know Thee in truth and glorify Thy blessed and most glorious Name for ever and ever. Amen."

When he had ended his prayer, he was carried on to S. Mary's. There, on October the third, 1226, in the fortieth year of his life and after twenty years of perfect penitence, he departed to the Lord Jesus Christ, Whom he had loved with all his heart, with all his mind, with all his soul, and all his strength, with the most ardent desire and with utter devotion, following Him perfectly, hastening swiftly in His footsteps, and at last coming in the greatest glory to Him Who lives and reigns with the Father and the Holy Spirit for ever and ever. Amen.

Mirror of Perfection, 124

There are other readings about the evening of St. Francis' death that speak of his requests to the friars: to read from the Gospel of John, to bring him some bread that they could break and share together, to have his brothers sing the Praises of the Lord to him, to be stripped of his garments as he was close to death so that he could die like Christ... These are accounts that are read on Oct. 3rd. But this story from the *Mirror of Perfection* was chosen because the blessing St. Francis gave over Assisi, could be read, I think, as a blessing St. Francis would want to give each of us who follow in his footsteps. Francis would want all of us to realize the *infinite mercy* and the *special and abundant favors* God has shown to us. Francis would want us to realize that God, in His goodness, has *chosen us for Himself* – so that we would become His *dwelling place*, and that from our lives His compassion and mercy, peace and joy would *spread abroad the fragrance of holy life, true doctrine, and evangelical perfection*. And so, may we be *ever mindful* of God's *abundant compassion*, know Him *in truth*, and glorify His *blessed and most glorious Name for ever and ever. Amen.*"

May the Lord of peace himself give you peace
at all times and in every way. The Lord be with all of you.
2 Thessalonians 3:16

Lord, I receive Your call to me to live the gospel life
with new determination. And I ask Your ever present grace
to help me be Your fragrant presence of love in the world.
Amen

Day 18
The Feast of St. Francis

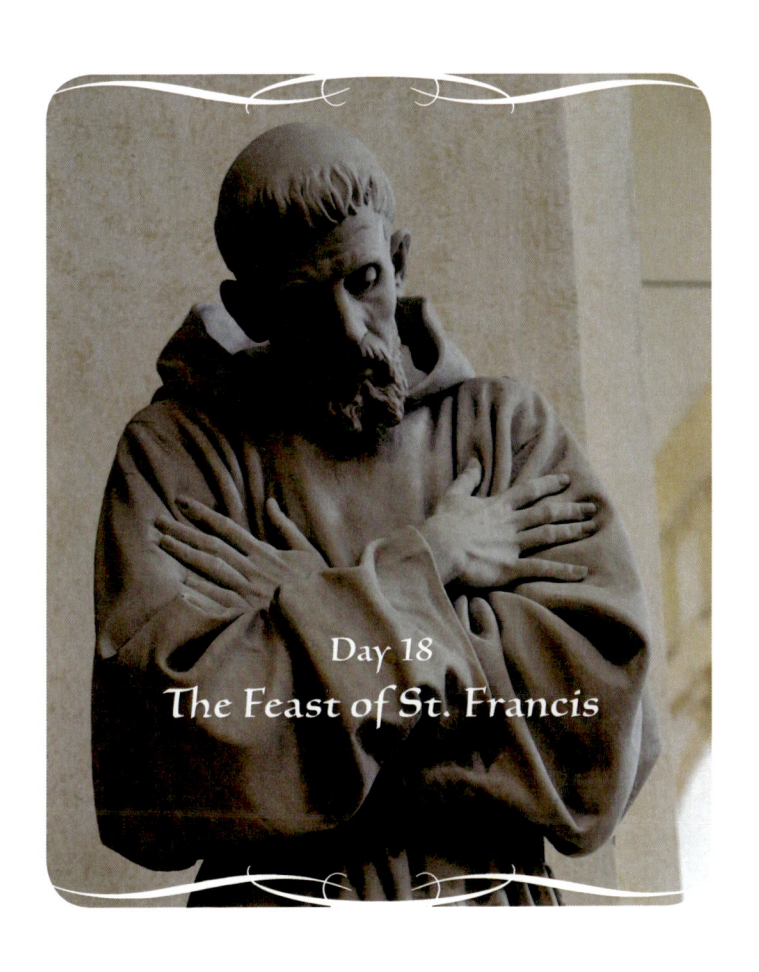

Our holy father left this world on Saturday evening, October 3, in the year of our Lord 1226, and he was buried the following day. He immediately became famous for the numerous and extraordinary miracles which were worked through his intercession, because God looked with favor upon him. In his lifetime his sublime holiness was made known to the world in order to show people how they should live by the example of his perfect uprightness. Now that he was reigning with Christ, his sanctity was to be proclaimed from heaven through the miracles worked by God's power, to strengthen the faith of the whole world. All over the world the glorious miracles and the wonderful favors which were obtained through his intercession inspired countless numbers to serve Christ faithfully and venerate his saint. Word of what was taking place, as well as the facts themselves, came to the ears of the pope, Gregory IX, so that he was aware of the miracles God was working through his servant Francis.

Bonaventure, *Major Life of St. Francis*, Ch. 15, 5

This servant of Christ, who so faithfully imitated Our Lord, gives us now a holy example to follow, prayers to pray and to live with our whole heart, and countless stories to inspire us as we strive to live the gospel life. Given St. Francis' love for the Lord, a fitting reflection to end this *Walk with St. Francis* would be to simply reflect many times over on the Lord, the Most High, Glorious God, whom Francis chose to imitate, adore, and praise at all times, in all circumstances, forever. These words of praise to God were written by St. Francis after receiving the Stigmata of Christ in his body. May his inspiration to write these words inspire us as well, to pray and praise God with our whole heart.

Day 18: The Feast of St. Francis

Praises of God

You are holy, Lord, the only God,
and your deeds are wonderful.
You are strong. You are great.
You are the Most High, You are almighty.
You, holy Father, are King of heaven and earth.

You are Three and One, Lord God, all good.
You are Good, all Good, supreme Good,
Lord God, living and true.

You are love, You are wisdom. You are humility,
You are endurance. You are rest, You are peace.
You are joy and gladness.
You are justice and moderation.
You are all our riches, And you suffice for us.

You are beauty. You are gentleness.
You are our protector, You are our guardian and defender.
You are courage. You are our haven and our hope.

You are our faith, Our great consolation.
You are our eternal life, Great and wonderful, Lord,
God almighty, Merciful Savior.

A Walk with St. Francis

Journal Pages for Your Walk with St. Francis

A Walk with St. Francis

Journal Pages for Your Walk with St. Francis

A Walk with St. Francis

Journal Pages for Your Walk with St. Francis

A Walk with St. Francis

Journal Pages for Your Walk with St. Francis

A Walk with St. Francis